The Discovery Books are prepared

under the educational supervision of

Mary C. Austin, Ed.D.

Reading Specialist and

Professor of Education

Case Western Reserve University

A DISCOVERY BOOK

GARRARD PUBLISHING COMPANY
CHAMPAIGN, ILLINOIS

Tad Lincoln
Abe's Son

by LaVere Anderson
illustrated by William Hutchinson

For

Pauline LaVere Thixton

with love

Contents

Tad Lincoln: Abe's Son

Chapter *1*

"Pa Is President!"

"Look, Willie!" Tad Lincoln shouted to his brother. "Look at Preacher Smith! He's throwing his hat into the air!"

Willie pointed to a giant skyrocket zooming upward. "Look, Tad!" he yelled. "There goes another big one for Pa!"

It was November of 1860, and Abraham Lincoln had just been elected president of the United States. His little home town, Springfield, Illinois, was celebrating.

All day the main street was crowded with happy people singing and dancing.

They shot off guns and firecrackers. "Hooray for Old Abe!" they yelled.

Two of the president-elect's sons, seven-year-old Tad and nine-year-old Willie, raced up and down the board sidewalks. Their big brown dog, Fido, ran at their heels.

Willie had a cowbell. CLANG! CLANG! Every time he rang it, Fido barked.

Tad had a toy drum. He beat it often and loud. BANG! BANG! The excited dog barked some more.

When it grew dark the tired boys started home. They lived in a two-story brown house not far from the center of town. No place in Springfield was far from anyplace else. Although Springfield was the capital of the state, it was still a small town. A few blocks past the Lincoln house, the farmland began.

"It looks like every house in town is

lit up," Tad said as they walked along in the twilight.

He was a lively boy with dark hair and eyes. His real name was Thomas. When he was a baby, he wriggled so much that his father nicknamed him "Tadpole." Now he was "Tad."

"I wish Bob had been here today," blue-eyed Willie said. "He missed all the fun." Bob was their older brother. He was seventeen and away at Harvard College.

Tad gave his drum a thump. "Ma says he'll be home soon to help us move to Washington, D.C. where presidents live."

"That's because Washington is the nation's capital."

Tad nodded. "Pa showed me a picture of the White House where we'll live. It's bigger than any house in Springfield. There's a real big yard where Fido can bury bones."

Willie began to look worried. "I think Ma is trying to find a good home for Fido here."

"No!" Tad stared at his brother in dismay. "We can't go off and leave him! It wouldn't be right. He's a good dog."

"We can ask Ma and Pa," Willie said, "but I think they've already made up their minds."

"We'll ask them as soon as we get home," Tad said firmly.

They found their parents waiting for men who were coming to see Mr. Lincoln.

"Get yourselves cleaned up, boys," their mother said. Her pretty face was pink with excitement as she hurried about the house. She wanted everything to look nice for the guests.

The boys peeked into the parlor where their father was reading. Pa looked very serious as he studied his papers.

"We'd better wait to ask about Fido," Tad whispered to Willie.

Later that night Springfield had a torchlight parade for Abraham Lincoln. A brass band played, and a long line of people marched past the brown house.

Each person held high a burning torch. Tad and Willie watched from an upstairs window. Fido watched with them.

"Everybody in town must be in that line," Tad said. "I guess everybody in town likes Pa."

"A lot of people all over the country must like him," Willie said in his thoughtful way. "That's why they elected him president."

Tad put his arms around Fido and gave him a hug.

"Don't you worry," he told his pet. "Willie and I are just waiting to tell Pa we want you to go to Washington too."

Chapter 2

To the White House

From then on, the Lincolns' house was full of visitors from morning to night. Tad and Willie hadn't known so many people would want to see a newly-elected president.

Some of the people were old friends who came to wish Mr. Lincoln well. Some were strangers who came to shake his hand. Some wanted jobs in the new government.

Newspaper reporters came to interview everybody, even Tad and Willie. Then they wrote stories to tell the nation what the Lincoln family was like. Messengers brought big baskets filled with mail. Artists came to paint the new president's picture. Photographers came. Mr. T. D. Jones, a sculptor, came to make a plaster head of Abraham Lincoln.

Bob came home from college. He looked very grown up and handsome in a tall, black stovepipe hat. Bob didn't like having so many visitors in the house all the time.

"Aren't you beginning to get tired of all this uproar?" Bob asked his family one morning at breakfast.

"No," said Tad, "Willie and I like it. HOORAY FOR OLD ABE!"

Mr. Lincoln laughed. "These rascals yelled that all through the campaign," he told Bob.

"TWE-EE-ET!" The sudden blast of sound made Bob jump.

"It's an election present that somebody

sent to Pa," explained Willie. He held up a strange looking object. "It's a whistle made from a pig's tail."

"Who would have thought you could get music from a thing like that?" chuckled Mr. Lincoln.

As the days passed, Tad and Willie waited for a good time to ask about their dog.

"Pa's always busy with visitors, and Ma is busy selling our furniture and packing," Tad told Willie sadly.

"I don't think there's ever going to be a good time to talk about Fido," Willie said.

The boys did not know that their mother had overheard them. She hurried away. Soon she returned, smiling.

"Boys, I've a surprise for you," she said. "You know we can't take Fido to Washington. He wouldn't be happy there.

He'd have to stay indoors most of the time, and he's used to running all over the country. I've found a good home for him with the little Roll boys. You've played with them, so Fido knows and likes them. He'll be happy there.

"Now for the surprise. I've just talked to your father. He's going to have the photographer take a big picture of Fido. You'll always be able to remember just how he looks."

Tad felt his heart sink. He looked at Willie.

Willie said slowly, "I guess he wouldn't like a big city. Remember, Tad, he's not used to a lot of carriages in the street. He could get run over."

Tad gulped. "I guess—I guess we'd better leave him safe in Springfield."

Willie nodded. "A picture will be the next best thing to having Fido himself.

We can look at it everyday."

At last the time came for the Lincolns to leave for Washington.

They rode on a train that the railroad company had decorated specially for the new president. The walls of President Lincoln's car were covered with red plush and blue silk. The furniture was dark and shining. At each end of the car were crossed flags with 34 stars. There was one star for each of the 34 states.

"I like this train," Tad said proudly. "They fixed it up real good for Pa."

"We stop too often," complained Bob. "People wait at every little station to see Pa. He must be tired of making speeches to them."

"I'm tired of waving to them," said Willie. "All those people crowd at the windows and yell at Ma, 'Where are the children? Show us the children.'"

"You always go to the window and smile and wave," Tad said. "You should get down on the floor as I do and hide."

"That's not polite, Tad," Bob put in. "The people are just being friendly."

Tad grinned at his brothers. "I'll bet you two wish you weren't so polite and could hide too."

It took almost two weeks for the family to reach Washington, D.C. By then, Tad was as tired of hiding as Willie was of waving.

Chapter 3

A New Home

"Come on, Willie! Follow me!" Tad shouted. His merry face was bright with excitement. "Let's explore!"

It was the Lincolns' first morning in the White House. Mr. Lincoln had taken the oath of office as president the day before. Now he was very busy with the nation's affairs. Mrs. Lincoln was getting the family settled. Bob was preparing to go back to college. Tad and Willie were free to do as they pleased.

"Follow me, Willie!" Tad shouted again.

Away raced the two boys. First they explored several parlors. Each was decorated in a different color. They were called the Red Room, the Blue Room, and the Green Room. Then the boys went to the huge East Room. It had handsome furniture and velvet carpets.

"This is where presidents have their parties," Willie said.

"We could have good races here," Tad declared.

Next, they hopped up the broad stairs and looked into all the bedrooms. Then they stopped to say hello to the president whose office was near the end of a long hall.

When they slid down the banister to the front hall, they almost bumped into the White House doorkeeper. He was a small, old man named Edward. "We're exploring," Willie explained.

"Why don't you explore the attic?" Edward asked. Perhaps he thought that would keep the boys busy for a while. He showed them the way to the attic stairs.

The attic was big and filled with old furniture, trunks, boxes, and barrels. "It's sort of scary up here," Willie said.

"Pooh! I'm not afraid," Tad said. "Look at all those wires on the wall. What are they for?"

Both boys began to study the wires. Tad pulled at one, and they heard the faint ringing of a bell downstairs. He pulled at another, and they thought they heard another bell. Willie went to the head of the stairs and listened, while Tad tugged at more wires.

"Every time you pull one, it rings a bell somewhere," Willie announced. They had discovered the center of the White House bell system.

"Let's both pull at the wires," Tad said.

Suddenly many bells were ringing. The boys could hear doors opening and feet running on the floor below.

"Whee! What a racket!" Tad cried with glee. "Let's pull them two and three at a time." They pulled hard and fast.

The laughing boys had no real idea of the trouble they were causing. With so many bells ringing at once, people were running all over the house, thinking that something dreadful had happened. Cooks hurried from the kitchen. Maids dropped their brooms and rushed into the halls. The president's two secretaries dashed out of their office.

"What is it? What has happened?" everyone asked.

Suddenly old Edward remembered. He climbed the attic stairs and stood in the doorway. *"Boys!"*

Guiltily, Tad and Willie backed away from the bell wires.

"Boys, you have the whole place upset. I suggest that you leave the bells alone hereafter," old Edward said sternly.

Tad and Willie went back downstairs, smiling to themselves.

"I'm going to like the White House," Tad whispered. "There are all sorts of interesting things we can do."

Chapter *4*

Four Friends

A few days later Tad and Willie were watching some goldfish in a tank in the White House sunroom.

"We could tie a string and a bent pin onto a stick and fish for them," Tad suggested.

Just then three visitors walked into the room—two boys and their sixteen-year-old sister. They were Bud and Holly Taft, and Julia. Their father was a judge, and they lived nearby.

Bud was a year older than Willie. Holly was Tad's age. The four boys took one look at each other and knew they would be good friends.

Bud and Holly stayed all day. They played hard and got dirty. They met Mr. and Mrs. Lincoln. They sat on the president's knee while he told all the boys a story.

"We've had the best time!" Bud and Holly said as they started home.

"Come back tomorrow," Tad invited.

Bud and Holly did. They often ate meals or stayed all night with the Lincolns. They began to spend so much time at the White House that they kept some of their clothes there. Sometimes their mother worried that they might be in the Lincolns' way. But Mrs. Lincoln said that she wanted Bud and Holly to come. Mr. and Mrs. Lincoln loved children. It made them happy to see the four boys romping together.

"Let's go sledding," Tad said one day.

"There's no snow," Bud objected.

"Oh, yes there is," Tad said. "It's not the kind we used to have in Illinois, but we can pretend it is. I'll show you."

He led Bud, Holly, and Willie to the attic. There in a big box was a great heap of small white cards, each with a name written on it. They were "calling cards" that had been left at the White House by callers over many years.

Tad grabbed a handful of cards and tossed them into the air. "See the big snowflakes," he cried.

All the boys began throwing cards. It was a paper snowstorm.

Next they needed a sled. The attic was full of old furniture. They took a chair that had no seat and nailed barrel staves on it for runners. Then they dragged it over the "snow."

Soon they were wadding cards together and stuffing the play snowballs down one another's neck.

"This is the first time I ever went sledding in an attic," Holly declared. "I'm glad you thought of it, Tad."

"Tad can think of anything," Willie said proudly.

One day the boys held a circus in the attic. Other neighborhood children brought their pet cats and dogs to be the "wild" animals. Bud and Willie dressed up like ladies in some of Mrs. Lincoln's dresses and bonnets, and Tad posed as "The Black Statue." Bud's and Holly's sister Julia helped Tad put on burnt cork as makeup and straightened the "ladies'" bonnets.

All the White House servants and guards came. So did the president. When he learned that Tad had borrowed his spectacles as part of a costume, the president thought it was a good joke.

Bud and Willie were usually quiet and well-behaved boys, but Tad and Holly were always thinking up new adventures. One morning they disappeared and were gone all day. Their families worried. Servants were sent everywhere to look for them. That evening a man brought the two boys back to the White House.

"We went to the Capitol Building and into the basement to see how far down we could go," Tad explained.

"We went down steps pretty near to China," Holly put in. "Tad dared me to explore around, and we did and got lost."

"There were rats down there, and it was real dark," Tad said. "A workman found us. He said we were in the sub-basement. That's the basement *under* the basement!"

"Didn't you get hungry?" Willie asked.

Tad shook his head. "A man who knew Pa gave us some supper in a restaurant. We had a lot of fun, you bet. You and Bud should have been along, Willie."

Mr. and Mrs. Lincoln hugged the two naughty fellows, glad that they were safe.

Tad and Holly kept right on getting into trouble. Once, they bombarded the president's cabinet meeting of serious bearded gentlemen with Tad's toy cannon. Another time, Tad ate all the strawberries that Mr. Watt, the gardener, was growing for a big state dinner. All of the boys, even Bud and Willie, raced and whooped through the White House. People said it sounded more like an army of boys than only four.

If anybody complained, the president just smiled. "Let the children have a good time," he said.

Chapter 5

War Comes

It was Tad's eighth birthday, April 4, 1861. The Lincolns had lived in the White House for a month.

The Taft boys came to eat birthday cake with Tad and Willie. Mr. and Mrs. Lincoln ate some too, but the president soon had to go back to his office. He was very worried. The nation was in trouble over the question of Negro slavery.

People in the North believed that slavery was wrong. They did not want it to spread to new states coming into the Union.

People in the South said it was each state's right to decide if its people could own slaves. If states were not allowed this right, the South would have to leave the Union, they warned. Finally, early in 1861, a group of Southern states had declared that they were no longer a part of the United States. They had started a new nation of their own, called the Confederate States of America. If the North tried to stop them, they said, they would fight. They began to raise armies and to vote money for guns.

Abraham Lincoln was against slavery, but he did not want war. He did not want the country to split into two parts. He tried to settle the problem peacefully. But feelings in both the North and the South had grown very bitter.

A few days after Tad's birthday, Southern soldiers fired on Fort Sumter,

South Carolina, a United States Army fort. When Abraham Lincoln sent out a call for Northern troops, the rest of the Southern states left the Union. The Civil War had begun!

Willie soon complained to Tad, "Pa never has time to play with us now. The war keeps him too busy. He's even worried that Washington will be invaded and the city burned."

"We ought to help him, Willie," Tad said. "Why don't we raise a company of soldiers to protect the White House?"

"That's a great idea!"

They enlisted Bud and Holly and other neighborhood boys. Mrs. Lincoln made uniforms for them like those of a brave New York regiment called Zouaves. The Zouaves wore baggy red pants, blue jackets with gold braid, and red caps.

On the flat roof of the White House,

the new company made a "fort." It had a small log for a cannon and several old rifles that no longer worked. There the company waited for the enemy.

"Let them come," said Tad grandly. "We're ready for them."

One day Tad and Willie were given a doll soldier dressed in a Zouave uniform. They named him Jack.

Jack turned out to be a bad soldier. He went to sleep while on guard duty.

"He's got to be court-martialed," Tad declared. "You know—the way they do real soldiers who aren't brave and true. We have to decide if he's guilty and punish him if he is."

Willie, Bud, and Holly nodded solemnly.

Jack was court-martialed. He was found guilty and sentenced to be shot.

"Bang! Bang!" cried Tad. "Now we have to bury him."

They dug a grave under a rose bush and buried the doll. After a while they dug him up.

Next day Jack deserted his post. Again he was court-martialed, shot, and buried under a rose bush.

By now the gardener, Mr. Watt, was furious. Those were new rose bushes he had just set out. The boys were ruining them by digging at their roots. What could he do?

Soon the boys came to bury Jack for spying.

"Boys, why don't you get him pardoned?" Mr. Watt asked slyly.

The boys' eyes sparkled. "Come on," Tad told them. "We'll get Pa to fix it up."

They trooped into the president's office.

"Pa, we want a pardon for Jack," Tad explained.

The president leaned back in his chair.

He looked thoughtful, as if this were the most important decision he'd have to make all day. "A pardon, eh? Well, Tad, it's not usual to grant pardons without some sort of hearing. State your case."

"You see, Pa, every time we court-martial and bury Jack, Julia complains. She says we get his clothes dirty. Mr. Watt is mad, too, because we dig up the rose bushes. So we want a pardon for Jack."

The president nodded. "I think you've made a good case."

He wrote something on a piece of White House paper and handed it to Tad. It said: "The Doll Jack is pardoned by order of the president."

So Jack wasn't buried. The rose bushes were safe, and Mr. Watt was happy.

Chapter 6

Sad Days

One hot July day the summer after the war started, a great rumbling noise came from across the Potomac River. The river flowed along the edge of Washington. On its other shore lay Virginia, one of the Southern states that had left the Union.

"Pa says there's a battle in Virginia. The big cannons going off sound like slamming doors," Willie told the Taft boys who had come to visit.

"The fighting's real close," Tad said. "I'll bet a lot of people are so scared they're leaving Washington right this minute." Bud and Holly looked scared too.

40

"Everybody tells Pa that he ought to send Ma and Tad and me away," Willie put in. "But Ma won't leave Pa, and Tad and I won't go either."

"We don't want to be safe if Pa isn't," Tad said firmly. "Anyway, there are a lot of soldiers guarding Washington. You know how many we see when Julia takes us walking."

"Tad's right," Bud said. He and Holly stopped looking frightened.

On their walks with Julia, the boys had seen the white tents of the soldiers spread all over the riverbank. There were hundreds of new young troops. They paraded with bands playing and flags flying. Every incoming train brought more soldiers and supplies into the city.

Now, thinking of all he had seen, Tad grew confident. "Washington is safe, all right. Pa has fixed that up," he said.

In late afternoon the booming of the cannon in Virginia stopped. Washington was safe. The fighting moved elsewhere.

People in the North had thought that their soldiers would win the war quickly. Now they knew it might be a very long war, and nobody could tell who would win it. As the fall went by, there was little good news from the battle fronts. Even Tad began to worry. He and Willie spent so much time everyday talking about the war that Mrs. Lincoln had to remind them to do their schoolwork.

She had set up a desk and blackboard in the big state dining room. She had hired a teacher. Bud and Holly studied there too. Of all the boys, Willie was the one who loved school best.

That December of 1861, a short time before Christmas, Willie had his eleventh birthday. For a little while the war was forgotten, and the White House was full of fun. Then, in the cold wet days that followed, Willie became ill.

For days he lay in his bed. Sometimes he was a little better, and sometimes he was worse. Then he grew very ill indeed.

One sad morning the doctor told the president and Mrs. Lincoln that Willie could not get well.

By now Tad was sick too. He lay in another room, tossing with fever. Anxious Mrs. Lincoln went from bedside to bedside.

"Where is Bud? I want Bud," Willie said weakly one day.

Bud Taft came. He sat beside Willie and held his hand. With his friend there, Willie could sleep. After that Bud seldom left Willie's side.

One midnight the president went to Willie's room. There sat Bud holding Willie's hand.

The president's worried face grew tender at the sight. "You ought to go to bed, Bud," he said softly.

"If I go, he will call for me," Bud said.

President Lincoln stroked the sleeping Willie's brown hair. Then he tiptoed out.

An hour later he went back. Faithful Bud was still beside Willie, but now Bud was asleep too. Gently the president picked Bud up and carried him to bed.

Tad was so ill he scarcely knew when Willie died. He could not go to the funeral held in the great East Room of the White House. Mrs. Lincoln could not go either. She too was in bed, ill from grief.

Bob hurried home from Harvard. He and his father stood beside Willie's casket. Their eyes were wet. Outside the windows a winter rain poured down, as if the sky too was weeping for Willie.

Chapter 7

Pa's Best Chum

It took a long time for Tad to get well. When he was strong again, he found that life was strange and different. Bud and Holly had gone away to school. Mrs. Lincoln's health was poor. Often she stayed in her bedroom with the curtains drawn, so that it was dark and sad there.

"Pa looks so lonesome and sorrowful," Tad thought. "Maybe I can cheer him up."

Tad began staying in the president's office most of the time. It was a big room with a fireplace, tall windows, a desk, chairs, and two sofas. Sometimes Tad stood at a window and looked through his father's spyglasses at soldiers drilling on the riverbank. Sometimes he played quietly on the floor beside the president's desk. If Pa needed a pen to write a note, Tad jumped up and handed it to him.

Tad began to understand more about the war and why Pa looked so sorrowful. The war was dragging on, with no end in sight. Many soldiers of both North and South were being killed. Pa grieved for all of them, just as he grieved for Willie.

"No wonder Pa works night and day trying to end the war," Tad thought.

When the president worked late at night, Tad curled up on the floor by the desk and went to sleep. Then his father would pick him up and carry him to bed.

"He can't be lonesome when I'm always here," Tad told himself.

Sometimes the two went shopping at Mr. Stuntz's toy shop. Mr. Stuntz carved fine little wooden soldiers, swords, and cannons. The president always bought many toys for his son.

One day Tad heard his father tell Mr. Stuntz: "I want to give him all the toys I never had and all the toys I would have given the boy who went away."

Pa's voice was so sad that Tad's heart ached for him and for the brother Tad missed so much. "We'll find an organ grinder with a monkey on the way home," he promised himself. "That'll cheer Pa up."

They did find an organ grinder on the street, grinding out music on his little organ box. A small, mischievous monkey wearing a red cap hopped and played on the man's shoulder.

The tall president in his black suit, stovepipe hat, and old gray shawl laughed heartily at the monkey's tricks. He laughed again when they passed another

organ grinder who had a bear with him. The bear danced clumsily to the music.

When they saw a candy man on a corner, they stopped to buy some.

Back home in the White House, Tad and his father got down on the floor to play with the toy soldiers and to eat the candy. Tad was right. He did cheer up the tired, overworked president. He was his pa's best chum.

Everyday the White House was full of strangers. Sometimes the front hall was so crowded that Tad could hardly push his way through. Many people waited to see the president. In his office the president would greet each one in his loud, hearty voice:

"Well, friend, what can I do for you?"

One day among the crowd, Tad saw a woman with tears in her eyes. He asked her why she was crying. She said she had a son in the army who was sick. She wanted to bring him home and take care of him.

"You tell my father about him," Tad said. "I'll get Pa."

He hurried upstairs to the room where the president was holding a meeting of government leaders. He knocked on the door—three sharp raps and two slow thumps. It was a code signal of three dots and two dashes that Tad had learned in the War Telegraph Office.

In the cabinet room the president heard Tad knocking.

"I've got to let him in," said Mr. Lincoln to the men. "I promised never to go back on the code."

He went to the door, and Tad explained his errand.

"My son, I cannot come now. You see that I am busy," the president said.

"I'll bring the woman up to you," Tad offered.

He did. The president listened to the sobbing mother's story and signed a paper which would bring her son home.

Tad helped many troubled people get in to see the president. His quick sympathy went out to everyone in need. Often he brought poor and hungry children off the streets and fed them in the White House kitchen. When his mother was well, he went with her to take gifts to wounded soldiers in the hospitals.

At Easter Mr. and Mrs. Lincoln held an "egg-rolling" party for Washington children. Tad saw a little lame boy there named Tommy. He found Easter eggs for Tommy. Then he got a chair which Tommy could sit on to roll his eggs down the sloping lawn. The lame child had a good time, thanks to kindhearted Tad.

Chapter 8

Mr. and Mrs. Tom Thumb

"I'll bet the White House never had a party like this before!" Tad told himself. On this wintry night in February 1863, President and Mrs. Lincoln were giving a reception for two unusual guests of honor.

Tad stood in the huge East Room watching the many ladies and gentlemen in their fine clothing. He thought Pa looked grand in a new black suit and white gloves. His mother had a flower in her brown hair. Her pink hoopskirt swayed like a bell when she walked.

The guests of honor had not yet arrived.

Tad could scarcely wait to see them. They were a newly-married young couple, and they were midgets. Each was only three feet tall!

Tad knew the midgets' history. Some years earlier a show man, Mr. P. T. Barnum, had discovered Tom Thumb. He looked like a small child, but he was really an adult. Mr. Barnum had put the little man in his circus.

Later Mr. Barnum discovered a tiny lady, Lavinia, and put her into the circus too.

The wee pair toured Europe and America as part of the show's exhibit of "wonders and freaks." They were favorites with audiences everywhere. They became the most famous midgets in the world.

When Tom and Lavinia fell in love, Mr. Barnum gave them a big church wedding. Now the Lincolns were having a party for them. The most important people in Washington were there. Like Tad, everybody wanted to see the tiny pair.

Suddenly there was a stir near the doorway. Mr. and Mrs. Tom Thumb had arrived. Tad's eyes grew round with wonder.

"They look like two dolls!" he thought.

Tom Thumb wasn't nearly as big as Tad, but he had a bit of a mustache. His wife was smaller still. She weighed only 29 pounds. She had brown hair and a round pretty face. She wore her white wedding dress.

The couple walked up to the feet of the president.

Up, up, they looked to his welcoming face.

Down, down, the tall president bent to shake their wee hands in his great one. He was so very careful, as if he were afraid he might crush their tiny fingers.

Tad rushed over to meet the pair. He hopped about them, beaming with delight. He dashed off to get ices and cake for them. Then the guests came to meet them.

Coming back with the cake, Tad heard the guests exclaiming. One lady said, "They are like two little creatures from fairyland."

"Nobody's talking about the war tonight," Tad thought with satisfaction. "Nor even about the great Emancipation Proclamation."

That was a paper the president had signed a few weeks earlier. It was one of the most important documents in the history of the country. It said the slaves in the South were set free.

"Yes," thought Tad, "this is one party Pa can enjoy."

By now the president had lifted Tom Thumb and placed him on a sofa.

Mrs. Lincoln lifted Lavinia to the sofa. They all chatted while other guests stared. Bob Lincoln was home on a visit from college. He stared too. Tad just couldn't do enough for these strange, wonderful little folk. He hurried to bring them more ices, more cake.

The president turned to Tom Thumb and smiled.

"See," said Mr. Lincoln, "you are the main attraction at the White House tonight. You have put the president completely in the shade."

The midgets laughed.

Tad spoke up. "Ma, if you were a little woman like Mrs. Tom Thumb, you and she would look like twin sisters."

The midgets laughed again. It was one of the happiest nights of their lives. And it was the happiest night the White House had known in a long time.

58

Chapter **9**

Tad's Pets

"The King of Siam wants to send me some elephants," the president said one day as the family sat at lunch.

Tad's eyes grew wide. Elephants! Not another boy in Washington had elephants for pets! He was sure of it.

"I had to politely refuse," said the president. "We'd have no use for them in this country."

"Pa!" Tad cried. "I could have ridden one!"

"You could ride a pony better," Mrs. Lincoln said. Tad wondered why she smiled as though she had a secret. He soon found out.

On his tenth birthday, April 4, 1863, his parents gave him a pony. Now he and his father could ride together through the streets of Washington. People soon grew used to seeing the president on his big horse, and beside him, Tad proudly riding the pony.

Much as Tad loved the pony, his favorite pets were two goats named Nanny and Nanko. They lived in the White House stable with the pony and Tad's rabbits. Mr. Watt looked after all the pets, but he didn't like the job. He growled that he was a gardener and not a zoo-keeper.

Tad often took his goats into the White House and hitched them to a kitchen chair. They made a noisy team as he drove them down the wide halls.

One day four ladies were sitting in the beautiful East Room, waiting to see Mrs. Lincoln. They were admiring the velvet carpets and fine furniture, when suddenly the door flew open. A boy driving a pair of goats dashed into the room.

"Gid-dap, Nanny! Gid-dap, Nanko!" yelled Tad.

Down the long room raced the boy and goats, past the great fireplaces and the shining mirrors. Overhead, the glass lamps shook from all the clatter.

The four ladies gasped with surprise.

At the end of the room, Tad turned his team in a swooping circle and raced it back.

"Get out of the way there!" the merry driver shouted to the ladies. Then through the door he and his pets raced—clippety-clop! lickety-lop!

"Well!" said the ladies. "*Well!*" It was all they could think to say.

Sometimes Tad tied ropes to the goats' collars and led them around like pet dogs. For fun, sometimes he butted the goats with his head. They butted him right back.

When he turned them loose to frisk on the broad White House lawn, they leaped among the flowers and chewed the bushes. Their sharp little hoofs dug deep holes in the newly planted grass. Mr. Watt hated those goats.

One summer day Tad went to the stable to say good-bye to Nanny and Nanko. "Be good goats while I'm away," he told them. Then he and his mother left on a trip to visit Bob.

Nanko was a good goat. She stayed in

the stable. But Nanny grew restless. She got loose and ran into the garden to eat the roses.

When Mr. Watt saw her among his prize rose bushes, he complained to the president. Mr. Lincoln had Nanny brought to the house.

Nanny was lonesome in the house. She hunted for Tad. When she couldn't find him, she went into his room and jumped on his bed. The housekeeper found her there in the middle of the bed, chewing her cud.

"Shoo!" cried the housekeeper. "Scat! Get out!"

Nanny got out. She didn't know where to go or what to do. For two days she wandered sadly around the big, empty White House. Then she saw an outside door that somebody had left open.

Outdoors Nanny raced, bucking and

butting. Now and then she stopped to nibble a flower.

A few days later the president wrote a letter to Mrs. Lincoln. He asked her to tell Tad that Nanny-Goat was lost and that Pa was very sorry.

"She disappeared and has not been heard of since," he wrote. "This is the last we know of poor Nanny."

When Tad came home, Nanko was safe in the stable, but Nanny had not returned. Mr. Watt looked almost too happy about the lost goat. Tad had his suspicions that sly Mr. Watt had carried her off.

"He knows what happened to her," Tad thought angrily, "but he'll never tell."

Something soon made Tad feel better. His mother received a letter from Springfield. It said that Fido was getting along fine with the Roll boys.

Then, when December came that year, Tad found a new pet-friend. Some people sent the Lincolns a big, live turkey for their Christmas dinner. Tad made a pet of the turkey and named it Jack. It followed him around the lawn and ate from his hand. The day before Christmas Tad rushed to his father in alarm.

"They're going to kill and cook Jack!" he cried. "They mustn't. That would be wicked."

"But Jack was sent here to be eaten this very Christmas," his father explained.

"I don't care," cried poor Tad. "He is a good turkey, and I don't want him killed."

Mr. Lincoln smiled at his warm-hearted son. He wrote on a card that Jack must not be killed.

Off Tad ran with the card, joyful now. Like Doll Jack so long ago, Turkey Jack had a pardon too.

Chapter *10*

Some Jokes on Pa

Both Tad and his father enjoyed the theater. The war had been going on for almost four years now, and the president had grown very thin and tired. Going to the theater was one of the few ways in which he could relax.

Once Tad and the president were at Mr. Grover's theater. Mr. Grover's young son, Bobby, was a friend of Tad's. The two boys played backstage almost everyday, and Tad knew the actors.

The audience became quiet. The house

lights were dimmed. Then up went the stage curtain. A patriotic play called *The Seven Sisters* began.

In the president's box, Tad squirmed beside his father. He was waiting for a chance to slip away without Pa noticing it. He had a joke to play on Pa.

Tad waited patiently until the president became interested in watching the play. Then he tiptoed from the box and went backstage. There he put on a soldier's uniform, which was much too big for him. When a chorus of soldiers marched out on the stage, Tad marched and sang right along with them!

In the president's box, Mr. Lincoln blinked with surprise. Was that Tad out there in a soldier's uniform? He leaned forward for a better look.

Grinning, Tad stepped to the front of the stage. An actor handed him an

American flag. Tad waved the flag in time to the band music and loudly sang a patriotic song:

We are coming, Father Abraham,
three hundred thousand more—
Shouting the battle-cry of Freedom...

The surprised president began to laugh. It *was* Tad! All the audience laughed, too, and clapped for both father and son. Tad was well pleased with his joke.

Another time Tad slipped away from Pa and appeared on the stage dressed in a beggar's costume. The president shook with laughter at the sight.

"I never know what I'll see when I go to the theater with Tad," he said.

This same fall was the year for another presidential election. Abraham Lincoln had been president for almost four years. Now in 1864, would he be reelected?

Some people thought not. They said, "The war has gone on too long. He should have stopped it and let the South leave the Union. He should not have freed the slaves."

Tad wasn't worried. "Pa will be elected again, you bet."

Election day was dark and rainy. Tad and Mr. Lincoln stood at a White House window looking down on the lawn. Some soldiers stationed there were voting. Turkey Jack strutted among them. Like Tad, the soldiers had made a pet of him.

"What's Jack doing down there?" the president asked with a chuckle. "Does he think he's going to vote?"

"No," said quick-thinking Tad. "He's not old enough." President Lincoln laughed. All day he told the story to visitors, while he waited to see if he would be reelected.

He was. Most people decided that the nation had a very good president who was doing a hard job well. They wanted the Union saved and the slaves freed. They voted for Abraham Lincoln for another term.

The next night Washington held a celebration for Mr. Lincoln. A crowd gathered on the president's lawn, cheering and waving lanterns. Again and again a cannon boomed.

The force of the explosions broke the glass in many White House windows. Tad was delighted with such a noisy celebration. Through the rooms he raced, excitedly checking broken glass.

"I knew Pa would be reelected," he shouted to old Edward, "but I didn't know it would be so much *fun!*"

Chapter *11*

Joy and Sorrow

Under a bright blue sky the steamboat *River Queen* lay in the harbor at City Point, Virginia. Around it were gunboats and other ships of war. On board were President and Mrs. Lincoln, and Tad. The president had come from Washington to inspect Union troops.

Tad stood on the deck, eagerly watching the shore. It was piled high with military supplies. Farther back stood rows of army tents.

Suddenly Tad pointed to a young

soldier starting up the gangplank. "Here he comes, Pa! Here comes Bob!"

A moment later a grinning Bob greeted his parents and hugged his little brother. He was more than just "Bob" now. He was Captain Robert Todd Lincoln, an officer in the Union Army.

It was a happy family meeting, made still happier because they knew the war was almost over. The North had won many victories by this spring of 1865.

Tad could scarcely take his eyes off his captain brother. He stared admiringly at Bob's blue uniform with the shiny brass buttons.

"You look real grand," he told Bob.

For several days the *River Queen* lay in the harbor while the president met with the troops. Tad had a fine time making friends with the soldiers. At times Tad could hear the far-off booming of cannon and see the flashes of gunfire. There was still fighting going on. Then came a great victory for the North. Union troops took the city of Richmond, Virginia. It had been the capital of the Confederate States. The war was almost at an end!

The following day President Lincoln took Tad with him when he went to visit Richmond. It happened to be Tad's twelfth birthday. Down the hot, dusty streets they walked. Everywhere crowds of freed slaves greeted them.

"Glory, hallelujah!" the freed people cried when they saw Abraham Lincoln. Some fell to their knees before him. "Bless you, Mr. Lincoln," they said.

Tad felt his heart swell with love and pride for Pa.

A few days later, when the Lincolns returned to Washington, they found a victory celebration going on. There were

flags and bonfires and bands everywhere.

"It's like a giant party!" exclaimed Tad.

At night the president was to make a speech, and many people gathered on the White House lawn to hear him. Suddenly laughter rippled over the crowd. People began to point upward.

There in a second-floor window stood a merry Tad. He was waving a Confederate flag from the window.

Old Edward came to the window. He grabbed the seat of Tad's pants and hauled him away. The crowd roared with glee.

"That Tad!" the people laughed. "What will he think of next!"

A few nights later, when President and Mrs. Lincoln sat in a theater, a shot rang out. The president slumped in his chair. He had been shot in the head by an assassin named John Wilkes Booth.

The next morning a sad and lonely Tad wandered through the big White House. At last he went to his father's empty office and looked out the window. A cold rain was falling. He could not believe that so few hours ago the streets had been gay with bonfires and bands. Now only church bells were tolling.

Tad fought back the hot tears that burned his eyes. "Oh, Pa," he whispered, "what shall I do with you gone?"

Then far out on the lawn, he saw Turkey Jack gobbling angrily at the rain. Suddenly Tad remembered another rainy day when he and Pa had stood at this window watching the soldiers vote. That was the day Pa had been reelected because he had done a hard job well.

A hard job! All at once the words took on a new meaning for Tad. Pa had been sad many times, yet he had done his hard

job. A strange, good feeling came to Tad. He had just asked Pa what to do, and it was almost as though Pa had told him.

"I am only Tad Lincoln now," he thought, "I am not a president's son. I must learn to take care of myself now. I must help Bob take care of Ma."

A manly look came over his young face. He turned to go to the room where he knew his heartbroken mother was weeping. He must comfort her.

"Yes," thought Tad as he hurried down the great hall, "I've got a job to do just like Pa had." And he knew that no matter how hard it was, he'd try to do it well. Just like Pa.